Splish, Splash,

ZooBorns!

by Andrew Bleiman and Chris Eastland

Most of the photos in this book were previously published in
ZooBorns: The Newest, Cutest Animals from the World's Zoos and Aquariums;
ZooBorns Cats!: The Newest, Cutest Kittens and Cubs from the World's Zoos;
*ZooBorns: The Next Generation: Newer, Cuter, More Exotic Animals from the
World's Zoos and Aquariums*; and *ZooBorns: Motherly Love.*

Ready-to-Read

Simon Spotlight
New York   London   Toronto   Sydney   New Delhi

SIMON SPOTLIGHT

An imprint of Simon & Schuster Children's Publishing Division

1230 Avenue of the Americas, New York, New York 10020

This Simon Spotlight edition June 2015

Most of the photos in this book were previously published in *ZooBorns: The Newest, Cutest Animals from the World's Zoos and Aquariums*; *ZooBorns Cats!: The Newest, Cutest Kittens and Cubs from the World's Zoos*; *ZooBorns: The Next Generation: Newer, Cuter, More Exotic Animals from the World's Zoos and Aquariums*; and *ZooBorns: Motherly Love*.

Text copyright © 2015 by ZooBorns LLC

Photos copyright © 2010, 2011, 2012, 2015 by ZooBorns LLC

All rights reserved, including the right of reproduction in whole or in part in any form.

SIMON SPOTLIGHT, READY-TO-READ, and colophon are registered trademarks of Simon & Schuster, Inc.

For information about special discounts for bulk purchases, please contact Simon & Schuster Special Sales at 1-866-506-1949 or business@simonandschuster.com.

Manufactured in the United States of America 0515 LAK

10 9 8 7 6 5 4 3 2 1

This book has been cataloged with the Library of Congress.

ISBN 978-1-4814-3098-2 (hc)

ISBN 978-1-4814-3097-5 (pbk)

ISBN 978-1-4814-3099-9 (eBook)

Welcome to the wonderful world of
ZooBorns!

The newborn animals featured in this book live
in zoos around the world. Get to know them through
adorable photos and fun facts written in language that
is just right for emerging readers. Your child might not
be able to pronounce all the animal species names yet,
but if you stay close by, you can help sound them out.

This book can also be used as a tool to begin a
conversation about endangered species. The more
we learn about animals in zoos, the more we can do
to protect animals in the wild. Please visit your
local accredited zoo or aquarium to learn more!

It is a sunny day
at the zoo!

This baby pygmy hippo
knows just what to do
to beat the heat!

Splish, splash,
baby pygmy hippo!

Who loves floating?
Sekiu, a baby sea otter!
To make it easier,
her mommy fluffs her fur
until it is full of air.

Splish, splash,
baby sea otter!

Valentine is a happy
baby American manatee.
He loves warm weather,
he loves the water,
and he loves his mommy!

Splish, splash,
baby American manatee!

It is bath time for Lily,
a baby Asian elephant.
She uses her trunk
to spray water!
It keeps her cool and it is fun!

Splish, splash,

baby Asian elephant!

This baby potbellied pig is taking a mud bath. Pigs love mud puddles. Mud keeps the sun from burning their skin!

Splish, splash,
baby potbellied pig!

Here is a fun fact about baby green sea turtles. In the wild, they hatch and head straight to the ocean!

Splish, splash,
baby green sea turtles!

Swimming is more fun with flippers and whiskers. Just ask a baby sea lion! Whiskers help them find their way in the dark.

Splish, splash,
baby sea lion!

Say hello to Nunavik,
a baby beluga whale.
Beluga whales are called
the canaries of the sea.
They chirp while they swim!

Splish, splash,

baby beluga whale!

These baby fishing cats have webbed toes that help them swim better than most cats. They look ready to dive in!

Splish, splash,
baby fishing cats!

It would be so fun to
play in the waves with this
baby bottlenose dolphin.
Soon he will learn
to do flips!

Splish, splash,
baby bottlenose dolphin!

Special thanks to the photographers and institutions that made ZooBorns! possible:

Cover:
CALIFORNIA SEA LION
Mary Kantarelou/Attica Zoological Park

PYGMY HIPPO
Zola
Dave Parkinson/Tampa's Lowry Park Zoo

SEA OTTER
Sekiu
C.J. Casson/Seattle Aquarium

AMERICAN MANATEE
Valentine
Wildlife Reserves Singapore/Singapore Zoo

ASIAN ELEPHANT
Lily
Michael Durham/Oregon Zoo

POTBELLIED PIG
Tiergarten Delitzsch

GREEN SEA TURTLE
Bob Couey/SeaWorld San Diego

CALIFORNIA SEA LION
PJ
Christopher Morabito/Seneca Park Zoo

BELUGA WHALE
Nunavik
Brenna Hernandez/Shedd Aquarium

FISHING CAT
David Jenike/Cincinnati Zoo and
Botanical Garden

BOTTLENOSE DOLPHIN
Mike Aguilera/SeaWorld San Diego